Dispensations in The Acts of the Apostles

I0164318

By Roy Ginn

ISBN: 978-1-78364-507-7

www.obt.org.uk

The Open Bible Trust
Fordland Mount, Upper Basildon,
Reading, RG8 8LU, UK.

www.obt.org.uk

Dispensations in The Acts of the Apostles

Contents

Page

Preface

Preface

This work aims to shed light on a most vital topic concerning the subject of the correct understanding of the Bible. I propose to examine closely the area of dispensations and their importance for the student of the Bible. The term 'dispensation' has been known for centuries but, for the main part, Christendom has lost a key to understanding the Bible by failing to recognise the importance of the dispensations to be observed in the Bible.

Part of the reason for the dearth of knowledge these days may be because modern translations do not use the word *dispensation*. But that is not so much of a problem in itself as the term really means an *administration* and can be explained in the light of that.

It is my hope in presenting this work that more believers in the Lord Jesus Christ will undertake to examine the Scriptures in the light of these things, and thus to learn to walk more worthy of their Lord.

A brief history of dispensational studies

A brief history of dispensational studies

Dispensationalism is generally understood in Christianity to refer to a theological system that teaches that biblical history is best understood in the light of a number of successive administrations of God's dealings with mankind, which it calls *dispensations.*

My research[1] on the world wide web has revealed that Justin Martyr (110-165), Irenaeus (130-200), Clement of Alexandria (150-220), and Augustine (354-430) all recognized dispensational distinctions in their writings. Indeed, to Augustine of Hippo is ascribed the phrase: *Distinguish the dispensations, and all is easy* or: *Distinguish the ages and the Scriptures become plain.* (There are various English translations.)

However, there then seems to be a gap until the 17th Century, when other writers demonstrated an understanding of the term. Among them were Pierre Poiret (1646-1719), John Edwards (1637-1716), and Isaac Watts (1674-1748).

The 19th Century, however, witnessed the advent of the Brethren Movement, where interest in the dispensations of the Bible came back to the fore.

---

[1] For details of the development of dispensationalism see *Approaching the Bible* by Michael Penny; see page 88 for details of this book.

The Plymouth Brethren movement was founded in Ireland and England in the late 1820s and was established in Plymouth in 1831, basically as a reaction against the established church in England and its ecclesiology. It became known for its anti-denominational, anti-clerical, and anti-creedal stance. While theologically orthodox, the Plymouth Brethren (J N Darby in particular) developed unique ideas regarding the interpretation of Scripture while emphasizing prophecy and the second coming of Christ. The theology of this movement became known as 'Dispensationalism'.

Dispensationalism became established in the United States of America in the latter part of the 19th Century. One well known proponent of the method was C.I. Scofield (1843-1921).

Scofield developed a correspondence Bible study course. This became the basis of the work for which he is chiefly remembered, the *Scofield Reference Bible*, a widely circulated and popular annotated study Bible that was first published in 1909 by Oxford University Press. This Bible teaches the theology of dispensationalism devised in the 19th century by John Nelson Darby, and it was largely through the influence of Scofield's notes on the Bible that dispensationalism became influential among fundamentalist Christians in the U.S.A.

The understanding of dispensationalism by the early Brethren was based on a system of belief that saw a distinction between the Church described in the New Testament and the promises made by God in the Old Testament to ancient Israel, i.e. there are two peoples of God with two different destinies, ethnic Israel (OT) contrasted with the so-called "spiritual Israel" (NT). They were able to see this as they adopted the literal interpretation of the Bible. Having been schooled in the Brethren movement for around 20 years, I am well aware of the teachings that are held on dispensationalism. They teach that the Bible reveals seven such dispensations (though I have seen variations on the number, but seven are noted in Scofield's reference Bible). These are as follows:

1. Innocence, (Genesis. 2:8-17,25), prior to Adam's fall,
2. Conscience, (Genesis. 3:10-18; Romans. 2:11-15), Adam to Noah,
3. Government, (Genesis. 9:6; Romans. 13:1), Noah to Abraham,
4. Promise, (Genesis. 12:1-3; 22:17-18; Galatians. 3:15-19), Abraham to Moses,
5. Law, (Exodus. 20:1-26; Galatians. 3:19), Moses to Christ,
6. Grace, (Romans. 5:20-21; Ephesians. 3:1-9), the current church age, and
7. Millennial Kingdom that has yet to come, (Isaiah. 9:6-7; 11:1-9; Revelation. 20:1-6).

It is interesting to note that they also see a correspondence between the periods noted above and the letters to the seven churches in Revelation 2 and 3. They suggest that the conditions noted in each period above are reflected in the character of each church addressed in that letter. Not all are agreed on the number of Ages being seven. Dr Frederick Albert Tatford (1901-1986), believed there to be eight dispensations (as he called them), and maintained that a new dispensation could only be established by means of a new covenant ("God's method with man", 1978).

Much as I admire these great men who faithfully sought to understand and expound the Bible, I have to disagree with their understanding of the term. They seem to have confused "Dispensations" with "Ages". The above so-called *Dispensations* would be better referred to as *Ages*, e.g. the Age of Innocence, the Age of Conscience, etc. as they clearly relate to time periods. My contention is that we have Ages, and we have dispensations within the framework of the Ages. The epistle to the Ephesians sheds some light on this:

> If indeed you have heard of the dispensation of the grace of God which was given to me for you, how that by revelation He made known to me the mystery … (Ephesians 3:2-3a)

> And to make all see what *is* the fellowship (dispensation) of the mystery, which from the beginning of the ages has been hidden in God who created all things through Jesus Christ, to the intent that now the manifold wisdom of God might be made known by (through) the Church to the principalities and powers in the heavenly places, according to the eternal purpose (purpose of the ages) which He accomplished in Christ Jesus our Lord. (Ephesians 3: 9-11)

In these verses we see a distinction between ages and dispensations. The dispensation of the mystery is part of the purpose of the ages and it is not the same thing.

Two other scholars from the 19th and 20th Centuries have contributed to a far greater understanding of the term. These are E W Bullinger (1837 – 1913) and C H Welch (1880 – 1967).[2]

The former wrote two books (at least) on the subject. The first one is entitled *How to enjoy the Bible*, and it lists twelve basic principles for understanding God's Word. Most Christians know they should study the Bible more but many find it confusing and hard to understand-much less to enjoy. This concise book on Bible

---

[2] 21st Century contributors include W M Henry, Charles Ozanne, Michael Penny and Brian Sherring. Information about them and their writings can be seen on www.obt.org.uk

study is a handbook for discovery, understanding, and enjoyment of the truths revealed in the Word of God. It is a guide to learn how to let Scripture interpret Scripture.

The second book on the subject is entitled *Foundations of Dispensational Truth*.[3] This is Dr. Bullinger's last book and is his definitive work on the subject of dispensationalism. It covers the ministries of the prophets, the Son of God, those that heard Christ, and the ministry of Paul, the Apostle to the Gentiles. He comments on the Gospels and the Pauline epistles and has a lengthy section on the Acts of the Apostles, followed by one explaining why miraculous signs of the Acts period ceased (one of the important outcomes of the change in dispensation).

Mr C H Welch wrote much on the subject of dispensations, as well as speaking much on the subject at the Chapel of the Opened Book in London, and in many other places beside. The understanding of dispensations and of the structures of the books of the Bible underpinned all his works. His most comprehensive work is entitled *An Alphabetical Analysis*. This is contained in ten volumes and the first five relate to dispensational truth. The other five deal with doctrinal, prophetic and practical truth.

---

[3] Published by The Open Bible Trust: see page 90 for details of this book

Towards an understanding of "dispensations"

Towards an understanding of "dispensations"

The word *Dispensation (Stewardship)* occurs nine times in the English of the New King James Version. In each case it is a translation of the Greek word *oikonomia*. This word has to do with the management of household affairs and is variously translated as *stewardship* or *administration* as well as *dispensation*. It is a combination of *oikos* (house), and *nomos* (administration or management). It comes through our language in the words Economy and Economics.

The nine occurrences of are as follows:

1. Luke 16:2   rendered   Stewardship
2. Luke 16:2   rendered   Stewardship
3. Luke 16:2   rendered   Stewardship
4. 1 Corinthians 9:17   rendered   Stewardship
5. Ephesians 1:10   rendered   Dispensation
6. Ephesians 3:2   rendered   Dispensation
7. Ephesians 3:9   rendered   Fellowship
8. Colossians 1:25   rendered   Stewardship
9. Titus 1:7   rendered   Steward

The first occurrence is found in Luke 16:1-4:

He also said to His disciples: "There was a certain rich man who had a steward, and an accusation was brought to him that this man was wasting his goods. So he called him and said to him, 'What is this I hear about you? Give an account of your stewardship, for you can no longer be steward.' Then the steward said within himself, 'What shall I do? For my master is taking the stewardship away from me. I cannot dig; I am ashamed to beg. I have resolved what to do, that when I am put out of the stewardship, they may receive me into their houses.'"

A close inspection of the verses in their context will reveal that it refers to a responsible office or ministry entrusted to a person (the Steward or Administrator) by a higher authority. This idea can be seen also in the following verses:

> For if I do this willingly, I have a reward; but if against my will, I have been entrusted with a stewardship. (1 Corinthians 9:17)

> If indeed you have heard of the dispensation of the grace of God which was given to me for you (Ephesians 3:2)

> … I became a minister according to the stewardship from God which was given to me for you, to fulfill the word of God. (Colossians 1:25)

The other three references appear to show a slightly different shade of meaning in that they seem to refer more to a particular way of administration used by God in the dispensation. Ephesians 1 is most poignant here:

that in the dispensation of the fullness of the times He might gather together in one all things in Christ, both which are in heaven, and which are on earth - in him. (Ephesians 1:10)

This refers to the action to be taken by God Himself. He will do the gathering-in.

So, we can see from the above references that there are four basic components of a dispensation: -

- **The Master.** This is the owner of the household and thus is the one who has all authority over the house, by virtue of ownership. He imposes the rules of the household and selects who will be the Steward.

- **The Steward (Administrator/Manager).** This is the one whose role is to manage the household on behalf of the owner. This person has all authority given to him by delegation, but he is still accountable to the Master who has the overall authority.

- **The Household.** This describes the property and resources (including the people) that belong to the Master and are subject to the authority of the Steward.

- **The Rules of the Household**. These are the regulations and laws given by the Master to the Steward, which are to be applied by the latter in order that the household may be governed in the manner so desired by the Master.

We have an example of these four components of a dispensation in the account of Joseph and Pharaoh in Genesis 41. When Joseph was in prison in Egypt, Pharaoh had a dream which neither he nor his magicians and wise men could understand. The Chief Butler recounted to Pharaoh that whilst he was in prison, along with the Chief Baker, they both had dreams which they could not interpret. He told Pharaoh that there was a young Hebrew in the prison with them who was able to interpret their dreams, and that each interpretation was fulfilled, just as the young man had said. This young man was Joseph. As a result of this, Pharaoh summoned Joseph, and he was brought before him to explain the meaning to him. Not only did Joseph interpret the dream, but he also told Pharaoh what needed to be done to prepare for the events foretold in the dream. How did Pharaoh react to what he was told?

> Then Pharaoh said to Joseph, "Inasmuch as God has shown you all this, there is no one as discerning and wise as you. You shall be over my house, and all my people shall be ruled according to your word; only in regard to the throne will I be greater than you." And Pharaoh said to Joseph, "See, I have set you over all the land of Egypt." Then Pharaoh took his signet ring off his hand and put it on Joseph's hand; and he clothed him in garments of fine linen and put a gold chain around his neck. And he had him ride in the second chariot which he had; and they cried out before him, "Bow the knee!" So he set him over all the land of Egypt. Pharaoh also said to Joseph, "I *am* Pharaoh, and without your consent no man may lift his hand or foot in all the land of Egypt.". (Genesis 41:39-44)

So we have the four components:

- The Master – Pharaoh
- The Steward – Joseph
- The Household – Pharaoh's house, all the people of Pharaoh, all the land of Egypt

- The Rules of the Household – The laws of Egypt administered by Joseph's word

Under God's providence, Joseph had been sold into slavery by his brothers. Their motivation for doing so was evil, but Joseph told them, when he was reunited with them, that God meant it for good, to save many peoples' lives during the famine that was due to come upon them (Genesis 45:5).

The same outworking of the components can be seen in Ephesians:

… if indeed you have heard of the dispensation of the grace of God which was given to me for you. (Ephesians 3:2)

- The Master – God
- The Steward – Paul
- The Household – "You". Initially to the Ephesians[4] but also to all those who are of the household of God (Ephesians 3:9)
- The Rules of the Household – The grace of God which was given to Paul (Ephesians 3:2)

So once again we can see that the pattern holds, and we shall refer again to this format as we look deeper into the subject.

---

[4] It is widely accepted that the Ephesian epistle was written to all believers, with the words "to Ephesus" being a subsequent addition.

Practical applications

Practical applications

The definition I have proposed does not include any reference to time. A dispensation may indeed cover a period of time (as the household relates to people, and people are always subject to time), but it is not a primary consideration when looking at the meaning of the word.

Now if we were to look at all the dispensations of the Bible, then that would mean looking at all households, all masters, and all stewards. That is not the purpose of this study. I want to narrow the search to dispensations where God is the Master. In these dispensations you see specific revelations being given to various companies of God's people, according to His own purpose.

Despite having a working definition, it is not always easy to determine where one dispensation may end and another one may begin; there is also the possibility of more than one dispensation being in operation during any of the Ages. However, for us today it is important to understand which dispensation we are now in, as it governs the rules by which the household that we are part of is administered.

It is not honouring God to obey rules that God required of people in a different dispensation, which are not applicable to us and apply them to the dispensation in operation today. For instance, when did you last offer a burnt offering to God, or wave a sheaf offering before Him? The answer should be obvious. We do not do these things today because they belong to a previous dispensation. In Romans we read:-

> What advantage then has the Jew, or what is the profit of circumcision? Much in every way! Chiefly because to them were committed the oracles of God. (Romans 3:1-2)

We would not attempt to keep the law or to practise circumcision today, because these were given to the people of Israel. They correspond to the *Rules of the Household* component of our definition of a dispensation, and we should not try to include ourselves in that household.

The important question is what dispensation, or dispensations, apply today? The answer to this question will govern the principles we absorb and teach to others and the practices we are expected to adhere to today. Thus, the answer to that question has a direct bearing on our walk here on earth.

Problems exist over different views of what is relevant today. Some Christians believe that the gifts of the Spirit, as detailed in 1 Corinthians 12, are truth for today and we should expect to see these things in today's world. Others believe that these gifts ceased when the twelve Apostles had died. But is either view correct? How do we determine what beliefs and practices appertain today, and, if they are no longer applicable, when did they cease or change?

It is a prevalent belief today that the "Church" began at Acts 2, specifically on the Day of Pentecost when the Holy Spirit descended on the Apostles and on the believers. This, it is believed, signified the birth of the church, the so-called "spiritual Israel". This term is never used in the New Testament, and as good Bereans

(Acts 17:10-11), we should be examining the Scriptures to see whether or not these things are so.

So, if we have a change of household, then we have a change of dispensation. If the church began at Pentecost, then the household is no longer National Israel, but "Spiritual Israel". But is this correct? Before Acts 2 we had the following dispensation operating:

- The Master – God
- The Stewards – The Apostles
- The Household – Israel (Matthew 10:5-6; 15:24)
- The Rules of the household – The Law and the Prophets (Matthew 5:17)

So, did any of these components change on the Day of Pentecost as recorded in Acts 2? It would be a good thing to read the whole of Acts chapter 2 at this juncture as the events will then be fresh in your mind. You will then note the following:

- Master – No change: God (verses 11, 17, 22)
- Stewards – No change: The Apostles (verses 37, 42, 43)
- Household – No change: Israel (verses 5, 11, 14, 22, 36)
- The Rules of the Household – No change: The Law and the Prophets (verses 16, 25, 30)

So, a study of this chapter will show that there was no change of dispensation at Acts 2.

This is a most significant discovery as it will have such a profound effect on our understanding of truth for today. As such, we shall look at this event in more detail to see what actually happened and what it means to us today. But before that, let us just look at an event recorded by Mark:

> And they went out and preached everywhere, the Lord working with *them* and confirming the word through the accompanying signs. Amen. (Mark 16:20)

We are told here that after His resurrection and ascension, the Lord was still "working with them" (His disciples). So, if there is a change of dispensation here, we should expect some confirmation from the risen Lord that this is the case.

Prior to Acts 2: The Day of Pentecost

Prior to Acts 2: The Day of Pentecost

Before looking at the events of that momentous day recorded in Acts 2, I want to take you back to look at some events that occurred a short time before. When the Lord was on the cross, one of the seven sayings He uttered was:

> Father, forgive them; for they do not know not what they do. (Luke 23:34)

Who was the Lord speaking of when He said "they", and what was the answer of God the Father to this prayer of God the Son?

Peter informs us in Acts 3 that his own people, Israel, crucified Christ (verses 14-16), but that they did not know what they were doing (verse 17).

In regards to the prayer, if the answer was "No", and God did set aside His people Israel and start a new dispensation on the Day of Pentecost, then at least two problems arise. Firstly, the Apostle Paul who was directly called by the risen Christ to take His message to the Gentiles said to the Romans:

> I say then, has God cast away His people? Certainly not! For I also am an Israelite, of the seed of Abraham, of the tribe of Benjamin. God has not cast away His people whom He foreknew. (Romans 11:1-2)

So, do we have a contradiction in the Bible? If we say that God cast away the nation of Israel at Acts 2 and replaced them with a spiritual Israel, we have a contradiction, because the verses quoted above tell us that God did no such thing. The book of Romans was the last epistle that Paul wrote during the Acts period, and a number of years had passed between the Day of Pentecost recorded in Acts 2 and the writing of this epistle. So, if things had changed, how come the Apostle Paul did not know about it?

Also, if the answer to Christ's prayer on the cross was "No", then you have the spectre of one member of the Trinity overruling another. Surely this cannot be! The Lord Himself speaks out against such a notion:

> And He was casting out a demon, and it was mute. So it was, when the demon had gone out, that the mute spoke; and the multitudes marvelled. But some of them said, "He casts out demons by Beelzebub, the ruler of the demons." Others, testing *Him,* sought from Him a sign from heaven. But He, knowing their thoughts, said to them: "Every kingdom divided against itself is brought to desolation, and a house *divided* against a house falls. If Satan also is divided against himself, how will his kingdom stand? Because you say I cast out demons by Beelzebub". (Luke 11:14-18)

The Lord clearly stated that any unity which becomes divided will ultimately fail. So, if the members of the Godhead are divided, then it must fail also. If you believe in the Holy Trinity then you cannot possibly believe that God did not answer Christ's prayer and that He cast off His people Israel on the Day of Pentecost.

I also want to bring to your attention two events following the Lord's resurrection, and prior to the day of Pentecost, which have a most important bearing on our subject. Firstly, Luke 24 records some events that happened after the resurrection of the Lord. When He appeared to His disciples in the place where they were gathered:-

> Then He said to them, "These are the words which I spoke to you while I was still with you, that all things must be fulfilled which were written in the Law of Moses and the Prophets and the Psalms concerning Me." And He opened their understanding, that they might comprehend the Scriptures. (Luke 24:44-45)

Secondly, in the very first verses of the book of the Acts:-

> The former account I made, O Theophilus, of all that Jesus began both to do and teach, until the day in which He was taken up, after He through the Holy Spirit had given commandments to the apostles whom He had chosen, to whom He also presented Himself alive after His suffering by many infallible proofs, being seen by them during forty days and speaking of the things pertaining to the kingdom of God. (Acts 1:1-3)

It is important to note the order of two events here as they have a bearing on what happened next.

1. He opened their understanding that they might understand the Scriptures
2. He spoke to them of the things pertaining to the Kingdom of God, over a period of forty days

He prepared their understanding so that they may receive His teaching. How significant then is the event recorded in the next few verses in Acts:-

Therefore, when they had come together, they asked Him, saying, "Lord, will You at this time restore the kingdom to Israel?" And He said to them, "It is not for you to know times or seasons which the Father has put in His own authority. But you shall receive power when the Holy Spirit has come upon you; and you shall be witnesses to Me in Jerusalem, and in all Judea and Samaria, and to the end of the earth." (Acts 1:6-8)

Some believers today cannot understand why the disciples asked the question about restoration of Israel since they believe that the Kingdom had been taken away from Israel and given to "The Church". But these miss the import of the word "therefore", which relates what was happening at that time, to the previous events recorded above. It was as the result of the Lord opening their understanding and His teaching them the things concerning the Kingdom of God that they asked this question.

The disciples would have understood this to mean the restoration of the earthly Kingdom to literal Israel, as spoken of in the Old Testament. If Israel were off the scene and this was no longer a possibility, how come the Apostles seemed totally unaware of it?

They asked if He was going to restore the Kingdom to Israel "…at this time?" His answer basically told them that it was not for them to know the answer to their question. Not once did He say that they had made any error in asking the question. Clearly, they had not done so.

It was indeed a logical question to ask as a result of what He had taught them over the period of forty days, after having previously opened their understanding. They knew from His teaching and from the Scriptures that one day the Kingdom would be restored to

Israel as a nation. What they wanted to know was whether or not it would happen soon.

The Day of Pentecost

The Day of Pentecost

So, if the events recorded in Acts 2 do not represent a new dispensation, i.e. the so-called birth of the church, then what did happen at that time, and what was its significance?

Peter tells us what happened that day when he spoke to the assembled Jews:

> But Peter, standing up with the eleven, raised his voice and said to them, "Men of Judea and all who dwell in Jerusalem, let this be known to you, and heed my words. For these are not drunk, as you suppose, since it is only the third hour of the day. But this is what was spoken by the Prophet Joel". (Acts 2:14-16)

So to whom does Peter address his remarks to in this chapter? "Men of Judea" (v14 quoted above). He also addresses his hearers as "Men of Israel" (v22) and "Men and brethren" (v29). He was addressing his own people, the Jews. He then quotes to them from the prophecy of Joel chapter two. The book of Joel is one of the 12 so-called "Minor Prophets". However, in the Hebrew Bible the Minor Prophets are one book and the theme of this one book is RESTORATION.

The question His disciples asked the Lord when they had come together after the forty days teaching is most significant. "Will you at this time RESTORE the kingdom to Israel?" To restore is *not* to bring in something new! It is to bring back into existence something that had existed before. How could it possibly, then, refer to a church that some call the "spiritual Israel" when no such thing ever existed before?

Peter begins his quotation from verse 28 of Joel chapter 2.[5] But the previous verses in that chapter provide the context:

> So I will **restore** to you the years that the swarming locust
> has eaten,
> The crawling locust,
> The consuming locust,
> And the chewing locust,
> My great army which I sent among you.
> You shall eat in plenty and be satisfied,
> And praise the name of the Lord your God,
> Who has dealt wondrously with you;
> And My people shall never be put to shame.
> Then you shall know that I am in the midst of Israel:
> I am the Lord your God
> And there is no other.
> My people shall never be put to shame. (Joel 2:25-27)

So, when Peter said "this is that which was spoken by the Prophet Joel" (Acts 2:16), he was stating that the events that were occurring were the beginning of the time of restoration as promised in the Prophets. The events recorded in Acts 2:17-18 happened during the Acts period, but those recorded in Acts 2:19-20 did not occur at that time. What happened on the day of Pentecost of Acts 2 was just the beginning, and the rest of the book of Acts demonstrates

---

[5] For more on this see *Joel's Prophecy: Past and Future* by Michael Penny, published by The Open Bible Trust.

the progress which may have resulted in the full restoration of the Kingdom to Israel.

The obvious conclusion here is that The Day of Pentecost, as recorded in Acts chapter 2, did *not* signify the end of one dispensation and the start of a new one. There was clearly no change in any of the four components of a dispensation noted in this booklet (Master, Steward, Household, Rules of Household), and thus we have no grounds on which to say otherwise.

Following on from Pentecost

Following on from Pentecost

After the event of the outpouring of the Spirit on the day of Pentecost we read:

> Then those who gladly received his word were baptized; and that day about three thousand souls were added *to them.* And they continued steadfastly in the apostles' doctrine and fellowship, in the breaking of bread, and in prayers. Then fear came upon every soul, and many wonders and signs were done through the apostles. Now all who believed were together, and had all things in common, and sold their possessions and goods, and divided them among all, as anyone had need. So continuing daily with one accord in the temple, and breaking bread from house to house, they ate their food with gladness and simplicity of heart, praising God and having favour with all the people. And the Lord added to the church daily those who were being saved. (Acts 2:41-47)

This is the outcome of the remarkable preaching by Peter and the other Apostles on the day of Pentecost. Remember that those present at the Feast in Pentecost were all Jews, except for any Gentiles that had converted to Judaism (called "proselytes"). These people were the *first fruits of the harvest*, the beginning of the *restoration* of the Kingdom to Israel, as promised by the Prophets. But what was *the Apostles' doctrine?* It was the Lord's teaching:

He said to them, "I must preach the kingdom of God to the other cities also, because for this purpose I have been sent." (Luke 4:43)

The Lord was sent to preach the good news of the Kingdom of God to His people – the people of Israel (Matthew 15:24). This was His teaching both before His resurrection and after it, and after the time He opened their understanding to receive His teaching. There was no change in the teaching; no change in the dispensation.

Those who received the message had all things common, sold their possessions and distributed the proceeds to those that had need. Are there believers today who consider that Acts 2:41-42 is the pattern for today, practising this also? Note carefully that the verses above show that they continued breaking bread from house to house and did *eat their food*. Breaking of bread here does not refer to "Communion" or "The Lord's Supper". No mention of wine here. Breaking bread meant having a meal. They shared their food as well as having fellowship together in prayer.

The term "church" refers to a called-out company of people, and more than one "church" is referred to in the Bible. For example, Israel is referred to as "the church in the wilderness" (Acts 7:38. KJV), and the church referred to in Acts 2:47 and Acts 5:11 is foundationally Jewish and consists of those who had responded to the Apostles' preaching concerning Jesus the Messiah and concerning the Kingdom of God. This is not the same as the church which is the Body of Christ, which had not been made known by God at this point in time.

Acts 3

Acts 3

The following chapter (Acts 3) commences with a miracle. Peter healed a lame man who was asking for alms at one of the gates of the Temple. The man responded to Peter's command to arise by walking and leaping and praising God. He had received a far better gift than silver and gold. He now had the ability to earn those things for himself because his weak ankle bones had received strength. Those that saw this and knew that he was the disabled man who sat at the gate were filled with wonder and amazement at what had happened to him. Then all the people in the vicinity ran towards Peter and John to see the man for themselves.

Peter then addressed the crowd, explaining to them that it was not through their own power or holiness that the Apostles were enabled to perform this miracle. It was through their faith in the name of Jesus that this lame man was able to walk. Peter then told them what they should do as a result of what they had seen:

> "Repent therefore and be converted, that your sins may be blotted out, so that times of refreshing may come from the presence of the Lord, and that He may send Jesus Christ, who was preached to you before, whom heaven must receive until the times of restoration of all things, which God has spoken by the mouth of all His holy Prophets since the world began." (Acts 3:19-21)

Repentance is one of the key words of the Kingdom message. The people whom Peter addressed were "men of Israel" (v.12), and they were told here to change their minds concerning Jesus of Nazareth, to be converted, and then the times of refreshing and restoration would come, and that the Lord would return! How could this have been if God has cast away His people Israel and replaced them with "The Church"? Remember that the Lord was still working with the Apostles (Mark 16:20), so surely if they are getting it wrong, then He should be putting them right?

Heaven must receive Jesus until the times of RESTORATION, of all things spoken by the Prophets. So here we can see again that there is no change in the household rules. Were the nation of Israel to repent, then the Lord would return to restore the Kingdom to Israel as promised before in the Prophets. Can you see the import of this? The Lord could still return to set up the Kingdom if the nation of Israel repented at the Apostle's teaching and preaching. If Israel had already been set aside, this could not be even a remote possibility.

The Apostles make no mention of anything other than what happened to Christ, how these fulfilled the Scriptures regarding the suffering Messiah, and how the Scriptures concerning the restoration of the Kingdom could be fulfilled in the lifetime of the Apostles. The message is still the same as when the Lord was on earth. No change in dispensation is indicated.

It is vital to follow the literal approach to Bible study (let the words mean what they say). You may need to push aside all you have believed before and approach the words afresh in order to see the truth God has revealed in His Word.

Acts 5

Acts 5

The chapter commences with the story of Ananias and Sapphira who sold a possession, then gave part of the money to the Apostles but told them that the amount they gave was the full price they had received (v8). Having lied to the Holy Spirit (v3), both husband and wife lost their lives. As a result of those events, we read:

> So great fear came upon all the church and upon all who heard these things. And through the hands of the apostles many signs and wonders were done among the people. And they were all with one accord in Solomon's Porch. (Acts 5:11-12)

We see here echoes of things that happened on the day of Pentecost (Acts 2:43-44). So again we see the Apostles continuing to do as they did on the day of Pentecost. These events angered the high priest who had the Apostles put in prison. But in the night an angel of the Lord opened the prison doors, brought them out and told them to go to *The Temple* and speak to *The People* (Israel) all the words of this life (verse 20). The Apostles obeyed this instruction, and when the officers went to the prison they found it securely shut, but the Apostles were not there. When it was discovered that they were preaching in the Temple, the Captain went to bring them to the high priest, who questioned them thus:

> "Did we not strictly command you not to teach in this name? And look, you have filled Jerusalem with your doctrine, and intend to bring this Man's blood on us!" But Peter and the *other* apostles answered and said: "We ought to obey God rather than men. The God of our fathers raised

up Jesus whom you murdered by hanging on a tree. Him God has exalted to His right hand *to be* Prince and Saviour, to give repentance to Israel and forgiveness of sins. And we are His witnesses to these things, and *so* also *is* the Holy Spirit whom God has given to those who obey Him." (Acts 5: 28-32)

Note the clear words above. God exalted Christ to be Prince and Saviour, to give repentance *to Israel*. This can only mean the nation of Israel. No mention of a spiritual Israel or a Gentile church. No, the same message is being given to the same people. Repentance was still required of the nation of Israel. They had not been set aside at the Cross, nor on the day of Pentecost in Acts 2. There is still no change in the dispensation at this point in time.

If we have been taught to believe that Acts 2 was the birthday of the Church[6], what do we understand to be the teaching of these events detailed in the last two sections?

---

[6] On page 64 of his book *Peter: His life and letters*, Michael Penny states "The Day of Pentecost was commemorated as the birthday of the nation of Israel, not the birthday of the Gentile church of today."

Acts 10

Acts 10

I am aware that a number of significant events occurred between chapters 5 and 10 of Acts, not least being Stephen's speech and his death, and the persecution and scattering abroad of believers that followed this. But during this time there is no mention of, or reference to, any new dispensation being brought in.

In chapter 10 we have mention of a centurion (a Gentile) called Cornelius, who feared God, gave alms to the people, and prayed regularly to God. This man received a visit from an angel of God who told him to send men to Joppa to locate Simon Peter who was staying there with Simon the Tanner. What follows is worth quoting here:

> The next day, as they went on their journey and drew near the city, Peter went up on the housetop to pray, about the sixth hour. Then he became very hungry and wanted to eat; but while they made ready, he fell into a trance and saw heaven opened and an object like a great sheet bound at the four corners, descending to him and let down to the earth. In it were all kinds of four-footed animals of the earth, wild beasts, creeping things, and birds of the air. And a voice came to him, "Rise, Peter; kill and eat." But Peter said, "Not so, Lord! For I have never eaten anything common or unclean." And a voice *spoke* to him again the second time, "What God has cleansed you must not call common." This was done three times. And the object was taken up into heaven again. (Acts 10:9-16)

In this vision Peter saw animals that would be unclean for an Israelite to kill and eat. Leviticus 11 and Deuteronomy 14 detail the clean and unclean animals. Peter was disturbed by this vision, coming at a time when he was hungry, but he did react as a good Israelite would and refused to eat anything unclean.

Peter saw the vision three times, and as he was pondering what he had seen, the Spirit said to him:

> Behold, three men seek you. Arise therefore, go down, and go with them, doubting nothing; for I have sent them. (Acts 10:19-20)

The Spirit gave answer to Peter's pondering. A vision seen three times and three Gentiles arrive to see him – sent by the Spirit of God. Why the need for this vision? The verses following supply the answer. When Peter went with the men to see Cornelius, he entered the house and talked with him and his guests. During that time, we read:

> Then he said to them, "You know how unlawful it is for a Jewish man to keep company with or go to one of another nation. But God has shown me that I should not call any man common or unclean. Therefore I came without objection as soon as I was sent for. I ask, then, for what reason have you sent for me?" (Acts 10:28, 29)

Peter needed a special vision from the Lord to make it clear to him that it was acceptable for him to keep company with a Gentile. If Acts 2 saw the start of a new dispensation, where there was no difference between Jew and Gentile, how come Peter, who was present when the Lord spoke to His disciples after His resurrection, was not aware of this change? Peter still believed he should keep the Law in all its fullness. This is a clear indication that he was not aware of any change of dispensation.

It was always part of God's plan to include Gentiles in the blessings promised to Abraham (Genesis 12:1-3), even though the *how* and the *when* and the *why* were not made clear to the Apostles. The Gentiles were grafted in to Israel's blessings, but were not called to be Stewards or Administrators. Their inclusion does not signify a change of dispensation in the Acts period. I fully concur with the conclusion of Michael Penny in chapter 22 of his book *Approaching the Bible*[7]. There he states

> ...a change of managers, or stewards, is of greater importance than a change in their rules and orders, or any alterations in the job they have to do. (Page 237)

Cornelius then explained why he had sent for Peter, and Peter responds by saying that he could see that God was no respecter of persons, and anyone who fears God[8] and works righteousness (as Cornelius had done) was acceptable to Him.

The Apostle Paul, whose conversion we first read about in Acts 9, wrote his epistle to the Romans towards the end of the period covered by the Book of the Acts. In this letter he clarifies the position concerning Jew and Gentile. In chapter 11 we read:

---

[7] Published by The Open Bible Trust; see page 88 for details.
[8] Cornelius was not a pagan Gentile, but was one of a number of God-fearing Gentiles. These attended the synagogues but sat at the back, or behind a screen, as they were uncircumcised, but they believed in the God of Israel, and, like Cornelius, prayed to God and gave alms (Acts 10:2).

I say then, has God cast away His people? Certainly not! For I also am an Israelite, of the seed of Abraham, of the tribe of Benjamin. God has not cast away His people whom He foreknew. (Romans 11:1-2)

Here the position of the people of Israel during the Acts period is made clear. God has not cast away His people! Paul himself was of the seed of Abraham and of the tribe of Benjamin. If a "spiritual Israel" was in view here, how come this is not made clear to Paul? He was not one of those who were with Christ from the time of His earthly ministry, nor numbered with the Apostles before Christ's ascension. Paul was called by the risen, ascended, glorified Lord to bear His name before the Gentiles, and kings, and the children of Israel (Acts 9:15).

So what was the position of the Gentiles during the Acts period? Paul clarifies this in Romans:

> For I speak to you Gentiles; inasmuch as I am an apostle to the Gentiles, I magnify my ministry, if by any means I may provoke to jealousy *those who are* my flesh and save some of them. For if their being cast away *is* the reconciling of the world, what *will* their acceptance *be* but life from the dead? For if the first fruit *is* holy, the lump *is* also *holy;* and if the root *is* holy, so *are* the branches. And if some of the branches were broken off, and you, being a wild olive tree, were grafted in among them, and with them became a partaker of the root and fatness of the olive tree, do not boast against the branches. But if you do boast, *remember that* you do not support the root, but the root *supports* you. You will say then, "Branches were broken off that I might be grafted in." Well *said.* Because of unbelief they were broken off, and you stand by faith. Do not be haughty, but

fear. For if God did not spare the natural branches, He may not spare you either. Therefore consider the goodness and severity of God: on those who fell, severity; but toward you, goodness, if you continue in *His* goodness. Otherwise you also will be cut off. And they also, if they do not continue in unbelief, will be grafted in, for God is able to graft them in again. For if you were cut out of the olive tree which is wild by nature, and were grafted contrary to nature into a cultivated olive tree, how much more will these, who *are* natural *branches,* be grafted into their own olive tree? (Romans 11:13-24)

So here we see the position. In a nutshell, some Gentiles were grafted into the Olive tree of Israel (to partake of the root and the fruit) because some of the natural branches (some Jews) were broken off due to unbelief. (We shall see more of this as we progress through the book of Acts.) There is also a warning to these Gentiles that they may be cut off themselves if they do not continue in His goodness.

Does this sound the same as being blessed with all spiritual blessings in Heavenly places in Christ? Does this sound like the "One new man" of Ephesians 2:15? Can members of the Body over which Christ is Head, be removed from that Body? No! This is a different relation-ship entirely from the one described in Ephesians and Colossians.

During the Acts period, these Gentile believers were grafted in to the blessings promised to Israel in order to provoke Israel to jealousy, and thus stimulate them to emulate the Gentiles who believed in Christ, and so be saved (Romans 11:14). They became partakers of Israel's blessings, which were material blessings in earthly places, and were the subjects of the covenants that God made with the Fathers of the nation, Abraham, Isaac and Jacob. There was nothing new being introduced here.

In Acts chapter 11 we see Peter in Jerusalem relaying the events of chapter 10 to the Jewish Circumcision in that city:

> When they heard these things they became silent; and they glorified God, saying, "Then God has also granted to the Gentiles repentance to life." (Acts 11:18)

The word *repentance* is a key word in dealing with the restoration of the Kingdom to Israel and here it is being applied to Gentiles. These were clearly being blessed alongside the Jews.

Acts 13

Acts 13

In this chapter Peter all but vanishes off the scene and we see Barnabas and Saul being separated for the work that God had called them to do. Saul's first miracle was to bring temporary blindness to a Jew (Acts 13:6-11; note Romans 11:25). In Acts 13:9 we see Saul is also called Paul, and that is the name used from then on. In the rest of the chapter we see Paul going into the synagogue at Antioch in Pisidia and preaching Jesus as the Saviour of Israel (v. 23). Some asked to hear him again and so he returned on the following Sabbath where almost the whole city gathered to hear them. This caused the Jews to be jealous and full of envy, but, sadly, they did not emulate the Gentiles and believe in Jesus (Romans 11:13-14): -

> On the next Sabbath almost the whole city came together to hear the word of God. But when the Jews saw the multitudes, they were filled with envy; and contradicting and blaspheming, they opposed the things spoken by Paul. Then Paul and Barnabas grew bold and said, "It was necessary that the word of God should be spoken to you first; but since you reject it, and judge yourselves unworthy of everlasting life, behold, we turn to the Gentiles. For so the Lord has commanded us: 'I have set you as a light to the Gentiles that you should be for salvation to the ends of the earth.'" Now when the Gentiles heard this, they were glad and glorified the word of the Lord. And as many as had been appointed to eternal life believed. (Acts 13:44-48)

Peter needed a special vision from God before he would go to the Gentiles. Paul did not as he was called to be the Apostle to the

Gentiles. It was always God's plan to bless the Gentiles through the nation of Israel (Genesis 12:3; 22:18; 26:4), and even though he was called to be the one to spread the risen Lord's message to them, he always went to his own people first in accordance with the commission given to him (Acts 9:15).

In the quotation from Acts 13:44-48, we see the first mention of Paul turning to the Gentiles after the Jews had rejected the message and we see that those who had been ordained to eternal life believed. These are the Gentiles who had been grafted in to share of Israel's root and blessings in place of those who through unbelief had forfeited theirs, and it agrees fully with Paul's argument in Romans 11:13-24. However, this is *not* the first entry of Gentiles into the Body of Christ, as expounded in Ephesians and Colossians as a careful comparison will reveal.

Acts 15

Acts 15

This chapter begins by telling us that men came from Judea to Antioch where Paul and Barnabas were staying, and taught the brethren that unless the Gentiles were circumcised after the manner of Moses, they could not be saved. Paul and Barnabas disputed with them vigorously, as they knew this was not the case. However, the company decided to send Paul and Barnabas to Jerusalem to meet with the Apostles and the elders to seek a resolution to the matter. Did the Gentiles have to be circumcised to be saved?

When they all came together there was again much disputing, and Peter, who had visited the Gentile Cornelius and recounted that God had told him to accept Gentiles and that through his mouth they would hear the Gospel, expressed his concern that some were trying to put a burden on the Gentiles that neither they nor their fathers could bear. (Acts 15:10; cp. Galatians 5:3).

Paul and Barnabas then had their say and were able to relate to those gathered the miracles and wonders that God had performed among the Gentiles and the people of Israel. After them, James, the Lord's brother, stood and gave his verdict:

> Simon has declared how God at the first visited the Gentiles to take out of them a people for His name. And with this the words of the Prophets agree, just as it is written: "After this I will return and will rebuild the tabernacle of David, which has fallen down; I will rebuild its ruins, and I will set it up; so that the rest of mankind may seek the LORD, even all the Gentiles who are called by My name", says the LORD who does all these things. Known to God from eternity are all His works. Therefore I judge that we should not trouble

those from among the Gentiles who are turning to God, but that we write to them to abstain from things polluted by idols, *from* sexual immorality, *from* things strangled, and *from* blood. For Moses has had throughout many generations those who preach him in every city, being read in the synagogues every Sabbath. (Acts 15:14-21)

These wise words were accepted by those gathered and a letter was written to Antioch confirming the judgement. James acknowledged God's work with the Gentiles through Peter who had recounted that the Spirit fell on the Gentile Cornelius and his household as they were, i.e. uncircumcised, and James confirmed that this agreed with the teaching of the Prophets. Thus the Gentiles were not to be burdened with keeping the whole Law of Moses or being circumcised as it clearly did not affect their salvation. Rather they were given four sensible rules to keep which enabled Christian Jew and believing Gentile to fellowship freely.

So here we have a clear distinction shown between the Christian Jews and believing Gentiles of that time. The Christian Gentiles did not have to keep the Law of Moses, only the four decrees suggested by James. The Jews, on the other hand, were still expected to keep the whole Law, as this would enable them to be witnesses to their fellow Jews who had not yet seen Jesus as their Messiah.

And when they [James and the elders] heard it, they glorified the Lord. And they said to him [Paul], "You see, brother, how many myriads of Jews there are who have believed, and they are all zealous for the law." (Acts 21:20)

Acts 26

Acts 26

In this chapter we have Paul appearing before King Agrippa, a man whom Paul knew to be an expert in the customs of the Jews. Paul gave an outline concerning his zeal for the Law from his early years and how he became a Pharisee of the straightest sect. He told the king:

> "And now I stand and am judged for the hope of the promise made by God to our fathers. To this promise our twelve tribes, earnestly serving God night and day, hope to attain. For this hope's sake, King Agrippa, I am accused by the Jews. (Acts 26:6, 7)

So here we see Paul talking about the hope of *Israel*, made to *the Fathers*, and he says that the *twelve tribes* are looking to attain this hope. How can this be if God had set aside the nation of Israel? How can Paul still talk about the twelve tribes? He then recounted his conversion on the road to Damascus where he heard the voice of Jesus speaking to him in the Hebrew tongue. The Lord answered thus:

> "But rise and stand on your feet; for I have appeared to you for this purpose, to make you a minister and a witness both of the things which you have seen and of the things which I will yet reveal to you. I will deliver you from the Jewish people, as well as from the Gentiles, to whom I now send you, to open their eyes, in order to turn them from darkness to light, and from the power of Satan to God, that they may receive forgiveness of sins and an inheritance among those who are sanctified by faith in Me." (Acts 26:16-18)

Here Paul reveals, for the first time, that when the Lord spoke to him on the road to Damascus, He said that He would appear to him again and reveal further truth to him. This further truth had not yet been revealed at this point in time (remember that God's purpose is an unfolding one), and Paul was to continue delivering the same message to the Jew first, until told otherwise. The Gentiles saved during this period were to receive an inheritance among the people of Israel, i.e. to be grafted into Israel's Olive, as before. Paul then proceeds as follows:

> "Therefore, King Agrippa, I was not disobedient to the heavenly vision, but declared first to those in Damascus and in Jerusalem, and throughout all the region of Judea, and then to the Gentiles, that they should repent, turn to God, and do works befitting repentance. For these reasons the Jews seized me in the temple and tried to kill me. Therefore, having obtained help from God, to this day I stand, witnessing both to small and great, saying no other things than those which the Prophets and Moses said would come - that the Christ would suffer, that He would be the first to rise from the dead, and would proclaim light to the Jewish people and to the Gentiles." (Acts 26:19-23)

So Paul confirms that he continued to witness to the Jews first and then to the Gentiles. His message was still the same, saying *only* those things recorded in the Law and the Prophets (our Old Testament). No new teaching here for a spiritual Israel or the Body of Christ.

Acts 28

Acts 28

We now come to the final chapter of the book of the Acts. Paul and his companions had been shipwrecked on the Island of Melita on their voyage to Rome. When they did eventually reach Rome, Paul called together the *Chief of the Jews* so that he could speak to them. There he protested his innocence and explained how that the authorities in Caesarea who questioned him, found no cause for death in him. He was constrained to appeal to Caesar because of the Jews' opposition to his release. They appointed another time to meet:

> So when they had appointed him a day, many came to him at *his* lodging, to whom he explained and solemnly testified of the kingdom of God, persuading them concerning Jesus from both the Law of Moses and the Prophets, from morning till evening. And some were persuaded by the things which were spoken, and some disbelieved. So when they did not agree among themselves, they departed after Paul had said one word: "The Holy Spirit spoke rightly through Isaiah the Prophet to our fathers, saying, 'Go to this people and say: "Hearing you will hear, and shall not understand; and seeing you will see, and not perceive; for the hearts of this people have grown dull. *Their* ears are hard of hearing, and their eyes they have closed, lest they should see with *their* eyes and hear with *their* ears, lest they should understand with *their* hearts and turn, so that I should heal them."'"

> "Therefore let it be known to you that the salvation of God has been sent to the Gentiles, and they will hear it!" And

when he had said these words, the Jews departed and had a great dispute among themselves. (Acts 28:23-29)

Here again Paul expounds the same message, persuading them concerning Jesus, from *the Law and the Prophets*. No New Testament was available at this time. However, when it became clear that they, the representatives of the nation, could not agree among themselves, they departed after Paul had quoted to them from the Prophet Isaiah. This came at a crisis point for Israel, as it did on two other occasions where it is used (Matthew 13 and John 12).

Paul then told them that God's salvation was *now* available to the Gentiles, without going through them (Israel) and that they, the Gentiles, will hear it. The Jews then departed. The Greek word translated *departed* in verse 25 is *apoluo*. This word is number 630 in Strong's concordance and it means to dismiss or discharge. The web version states that "This term implies the release (annulment) of an existing bond".

Clearly then it is at this point that God's dealings with Israel come to an end *for a season*. The gifts and callings of God are without repentance (Romans 11:29). So, God had not completely finished with His earthly people. Their full restoration is yet to come.

What has happened as a result of God dismissing Israel as the channel of earthly blessing is that He started to implement a new heavenly phase of His will. In this phase Israel does not have the first place. The Church which is the Body of Christ began here, at Acts 28:28 and not at Acts 2. In the Epistles of Paul written after the end of the Acts[9], we see Paul revealing the things that God said He would reveal to him at a later time (Acts 26:16).

---

[9] These are Ephesians, Philippians, Colossians, 1 & 2 Timothy, Titus and Philemon.

Conclusion

Conclusion

I believe that the activities of the Apostles after the Lord ascended were totally in accordance with what He taught them while He was with them, before and after His resurrection, as confirmed by Matthew 28:30. Just before His ascension, the Lord told them to teach those that they discipled to "obey everything I have commanded you" (Matthew 28:20). Therefore, there was no change of dispensation in the early chapters of the book of Acts, when the focus was on Peter and the Apostles that were with the Lord from the beginning of His earthly ministry. The message of the Apostles was still that of the RESTORATION of Israel. Peter made this clear in the early chapters of the Acts, and Paul continued the theme in the latter part.

Paul continued to go to the synagogues and preach Jesus the Messiah and to command the people of Israel to repent. After Peter learned the lesson that God had called Gentiles "clean", Paul was selected as the chosen vessel to take the Lord's name to the people of Israel, and the Gentiles (Galatians 2:7-9). During the Acts period Paul did take this message to the Jew first, but also to the Gentiles.

During the Acts period, Paul's message was in complete accord with the Scriptures as he said only those things which Moses and the Prophets did say would come. The book of the Acts contained no mention of the Body of which Christ is the Head, as that had not yet been revealed. It was hid in God (Ephesians 3:9), and not hidden in the Old Testament. When God hides a thing, no man can see it until God chooses to reveal it. There was no change of dispensation during the latter part of the Acts until the very end, when the Jewish leaders (representatives of the whole nation) were dismissed and their position of advantage taken away. The existing bond having been annulled, we see the time for a new dispensation to be ushered in.

The consequences are that we may need to re-think our approach to the Bible. The books written during the Acts period were written when the people of Israel were still God's people and should be read in the light of that fact, so that we look to learn what has been written *for our learning*. The Epistles of Paul written after Acts 28 were written after Israel had been set aside, and they can be seen as being written with us in mind, and thus the matters dealt with in these letters are to be viewed in that light.

I believe that Bible study will become a deeper and richer experience when we understand the instruction to *rightly divide* between what was written *for* us and what was written *about* us, and thus seek to walk worthy of the calling with which we are called.

About the Author

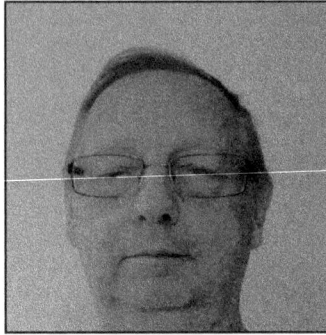

Roy Ginn was born in London in 1955 and spent most of his early life in Bromley where, as a teenager, he began to attend a church youth club and in 1969 became a believer in Christ. Two years later he left school and began a career in banking and moved to Birmingham in 1980. It was during his years there that he became acquainted with right division.

In 1988 he moved to Newcastle-upon-Tyne and after several jobs there entered the university, graduating in Accounting and Mathematics, before returning to the London area and continuing to work in the accountancy field. He lives in Essex with his wife Lynette.

Also by Roy Ginn

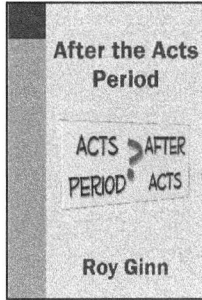

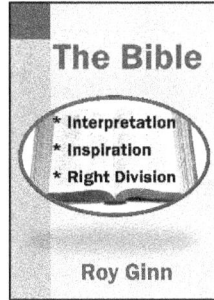

The Bible: Interpretation, Inspiration, Right Division.
After the Acts Period

Further details of these can be seen on

www.obt.org.uk

These are available as paperbacks from that website and also from

The Open Bible Trust
Fordland Mount, Upper Basildon,
Reading, RG8 8LU, UK.

They are also avaialble as eBooks from
Amazon Kindle and Apple.

They are also available as KDP paperbacks from Amazon

Also on this subject

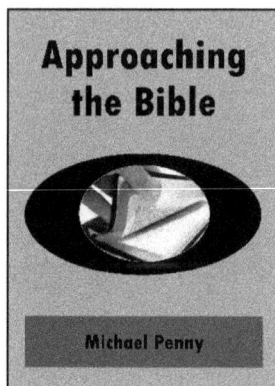

Approaching the Bible
Michael Penny

This book clearly explains how we need to approach the Bible if we are to make sense of what God has said. It does so in an easy to read style and with an easy to understand method. Michael Penny does an excellent job of following the advice of Bishop Miles Coverdale, which was contained in the first Bible printed in English.

That advice was based on asking such questions as:

- "Who" were these words written to, or "Who" were they about?
- "Where" is this to take place?
- "When" was it written or "When" is it about?
- "What", precisely, is said?
- "Why" did God say it, do it, or will do it?

After asking such questions, then we will have a better understanding of the Bible and can "Apply" that passage to our lives today.

****

Further details of this book can be seen on

www.obt.org.uk

It is available as a paperback from that website and also from

The Open Bible Trust
Fordland Mount, Upper Basildon,
Reading, RG8 8LU, UK.

It is also avaialble as an eBook from
Amazon Kindle and Apple.

It is also available as a KDP paperback from Amazon

.

THE FOUNDATIONS OF DISPENSATIONAL TRUTH

E W Bullinger

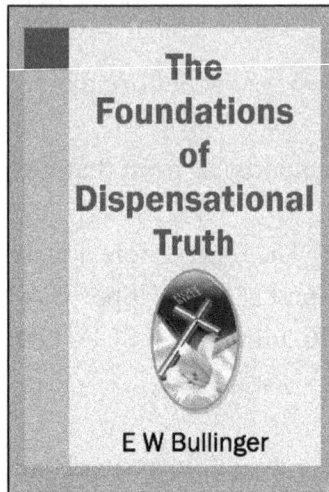

This is Bullinger's last book and is his definitive work on the subject of dispensationalism. It covers the ministries of ...

- the prophets,
- the Son of God,
- those that heard Christ, and
- the ministry of Paul, the Apostle to the Gentiles.

He comments on the Gospels and the Pauline epistles and has a lengthy section on the Acts of the Apostles, followed by one explaining why miraculous signs of the Acts period ceased.

A hard-back edition is available from **www.obt.org.uk** and from

The Open Bible Trust,
Fordland Mount, Upper Basildon,
Reading, RG8 8LU, UK.

A newly typeset book, well presented in an easy to read format, is available as a KDP paperback Amazon.

It is also available as an eBook from Amazon and Kindle

About this book

Dispensations in
The Acts of the Apostles

The term 'dispensation' has been known for centuries but today, for the main part, Christendom fails to recognise the importance of the dispensations which are easily seen in the Bible. It is the author's hope that in presenting this work more believers in the Lord Jesus Christ will examine the Scriptures in the light of dispensations, and so increase their understanding of the Scriptures and gain a greater appreciation of Christ Jesus our Saviour and so walk more worthily of our Lord.

Publications of The Open Bible Trust must be in accordance with its evangelical, fundamental and dispensational basis. However, beyond this minimum, writers are free to express whatever beliefs they may have as their own understanding, provided that the aim in so doing is to further the object of The Open Bible Trust. A copy of the doctrinal basis is available on **www.obt.org.uk** or from:

THE OPEN BIBLE TRUST
Fordland Mount, Upper Basildon,
Reading, RG8 8LU, UK